There is a body
　　without a heart
That hath a tongue,
　　and yet no head,
Buried it was,
　　e're it was made,
And loud doth speak,
　　and yet is dead.

A bell.

I am called
　　by the name of a man,
Yet am as little
　　as a mouse;
When winter comes
　　I love to be
With my red gorget
　　near the house.

Robin redbreast.

Sarah Morton's Day

A Day in the Life of a Pilgrim Girl

by KATE WATERS

Photographs by RUSS KENDALL

SCHOLASTIC INC. / *New York*

We gratefully acknowledge the following people for their generosity in sharing their time, expertise, and facilities, and for making Sarah Morton's story come alive: David K. Case, Executive Director, Plimoth Plantation; Dr. Jeremy Bangs, Curator; Dr. John Kemp, Manager of Interpretation; James Baker, Director of Research; Elizabeth Lodge, Registrar of Collections; Lisa Whalen, Assistant Supervisor of Pilgrim Village; Sarah Mann, Director of Marketing and Public Relations; Amelia Poole, who interprets Sarah Morton, her family; Regina Scotland, who interprets Julianna Morton Kempton; Jeffrey Scotland; Katherine Wheelock, who interprets Elizabeth Warren, her family; Stuart Bolton, who interprets Goodman Kempton; Peg Golden, whose artistic eye helped me see this story; Sandra Nice, who suggested this adventure. With gratitude to all.

The accuracy of this account has been verified by the curatorial and research staff at Plimoth Plantation.

*For Abigail Hebel Weir who will
lead our family into the 21st century.
—K. W.*

*With love and gratitude to my parents Jean and Jim Carson
and to my friend Thérèse Landry, pilgrims all.
—R. K.*

*For Jackie Duval, my sponsor
—Amelia Poole*

Library of Congress Cataloging-in-Publication Data

Waters, Kate.
Sarah Morton's day.

Glossary: p.
Summary: Text and photographs of Plimoth Plantation follow a pilgrim girl through a typical day as she milks the goats, cooks and serves meals, learns her letters, and adjusts to her new stepfather. 1. Pilgrims (New Plymouth Colony)—Pictorial works—Juvenile literature. 2. Massachusetts—Social life and customs—Colonial period, ca. 1600–1775—Pictorial works—Juvenile literature. 3. Children—Massachusetts—History—17th century—Pictorial works—Juvenile literature. [1. Pilgrims (New Plymouth Colony) 2. Massachusetts—Social life and customs—Colonial period, ca. 1600–1775] I. Kendall, Russell, ill. II. Title.
F68.W33 1989   974.4'02   88-35581

ISBN 0-590-42634-6

12 11 10 9   4/9

Printed in U.S.A.   36
First Scholastic printing, October 1989

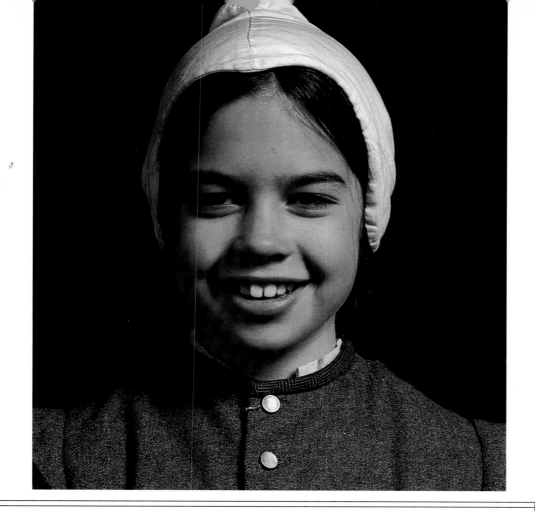

November 12, 1627

Good day.

My name is Sarah Morton.

My family sailed to America four years ago on a ship called *The Anne*. We came to seek freedom from the Church of England. First my family settled in Holland, where I was born. Life in Holland was hard for us, so we set sail for the New World.

My father died that first winter. This spring, Mother married Goodman Kempton. I am learning to call him father and am trying hard to earn his love.

Come thee with me. Let me show thee how my days are.

This is my village.
It is called Plimoth Plantation.

At sunup, when the cockerel crows, I must get up and be about my chores.

I put on my overgarments:

PETTICOAT

STOCKINGS

GARTERS

COIF

APRON

POCKET

PETTICOAT

PETTICOAT

WAISTCOAT

SHOES

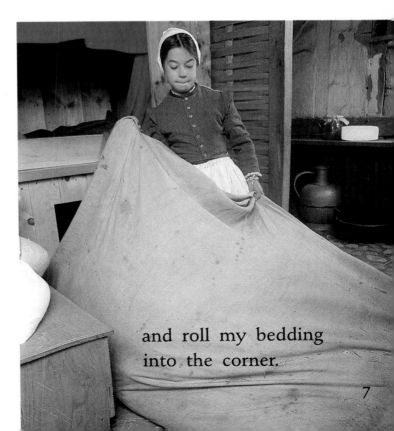

and roll my bedding
into the corner.

The fire is mine to tend.

I throw brush on the red coals to make them dance.

Mother and I make the hasty pudding.

I lay the table with clean cloths, bowls, and spoons.

I serve Mother and my new father first. I must stand at my place to eat. Perchance my new father will make a stool for me.

With the table scraps I have collected, I go out to feed the chickens.

Because I have forgotten to latch the pen, I must run our hens a game of chase.

At milking time, I find my best friend, Elizabeth Warren, at the pen. As we milk, we tell each other secrets.

Today I tell her of a dream about my real father. I miss him often, but I do not speak of him to anyone save Elizabeth. I do not wish to seem ungrateful to my new father.

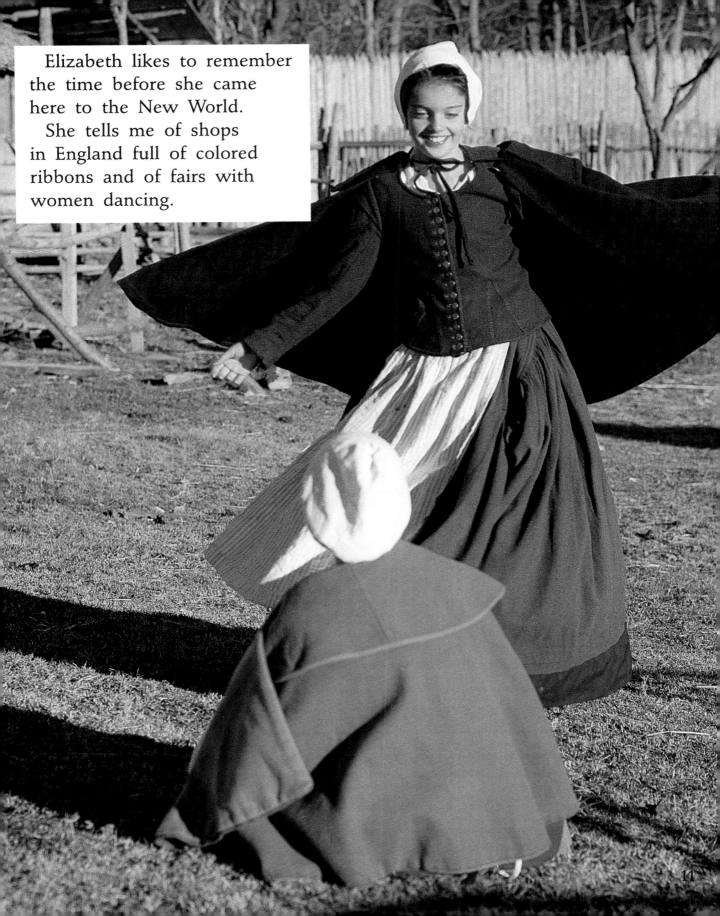

Elizabeth likes to remember the time before she came here to the New World.

She tells me of shops in England full of colored ribbons and of fairs with women dancing.

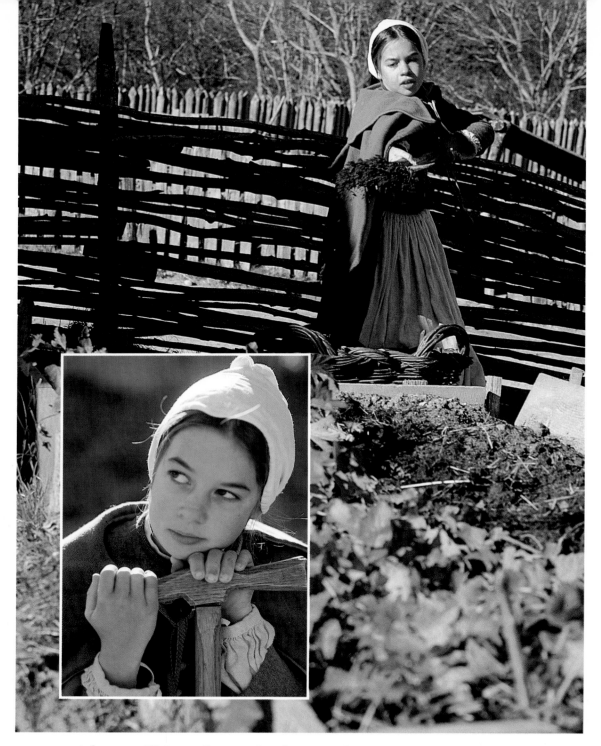

After milking, I muck the garden to make it rich for planting next spring.

The muck is heavy, and I must often stop to rest. "Hurry along, Sarah," Mother calls from the door.

Oh, marry! I am caught idle again.

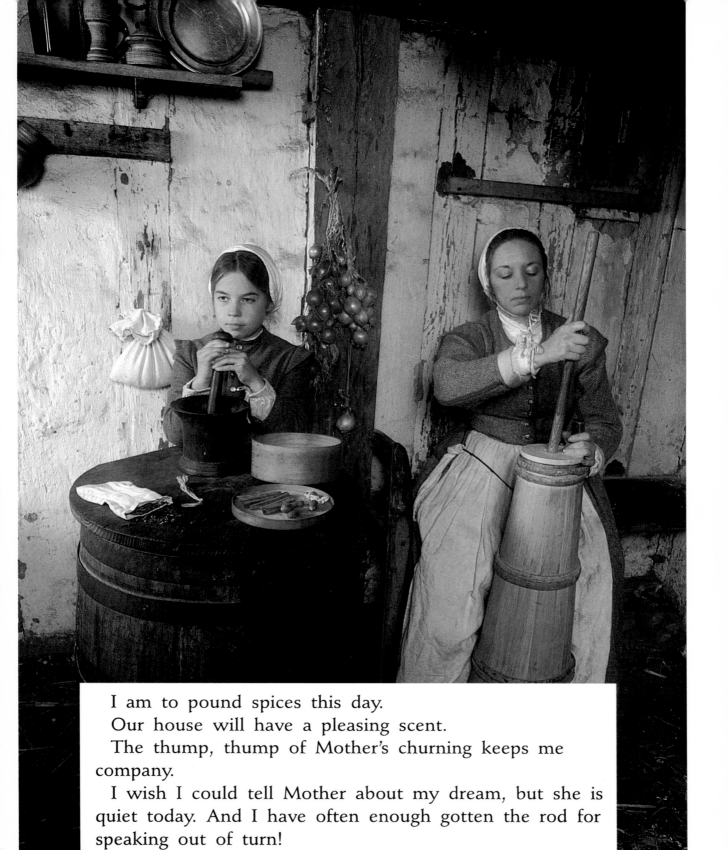

I am to pound spices this day.
Our house will have a pleasing scent.
The thump, thump of Mother's churning keeps me company.

I wish I could tell Mother about my dream, but she is quiet today. And I have often enough gotten the rod for speaking out of turn!

Next Mother and I prepare the midday meal.

17th Century Indian Corn Bread

Boil 3 cups of water. Stir in 1 cup coarse cornmeal grits. Simmer until water is absorbed, stirring occasionally. Cool. When mixture is cool enough to handle, turn onto work surface floured with ½ cup fine cornmeal flour. Work into 2 round flat cakes. Bake on floured cookie sheet at 400 degrees for ¾ hour.

(Here is the bread that Sarah made. But it probably would not taste very good to us today!)

When my new father comes home for dinner, he seems pleased with the rich pottage and warm Indian cornbread that we have made!

After dinner, it's time for my favorite task. I draw vinegar to polish the brass.

If I am patient and rub the salt and vinegar slowly, the kettle will truly shine.

Of a sudden, I hear a warning shot from the meeting house on the hill.

It means a ship has been sighted!

Perchance we will have some visitors on tomorrow's tide. I pray that they won't be people who wish us harm.

Mother says I may fetch Elizabeth.

We run to the top of the hill to see the ship.

But it is still a tiny speck at sea.

I dare not wait to see more.

It is time for my lessons.

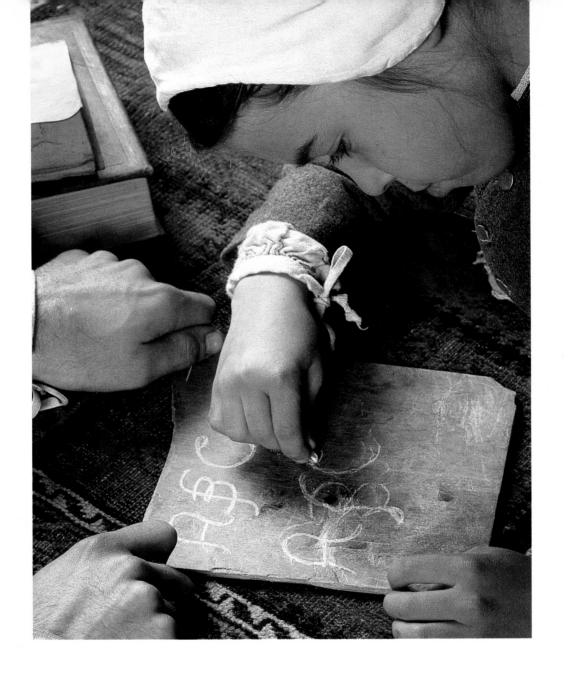

My new father thinks I show a talent for learning!

I am grateful, for in many families girls are not spared from their chores for lessons.

My fingers are clumsy around the chalk, but it gets easier.

Some day I may be able to read Mother the letters she gets from her relations in England!

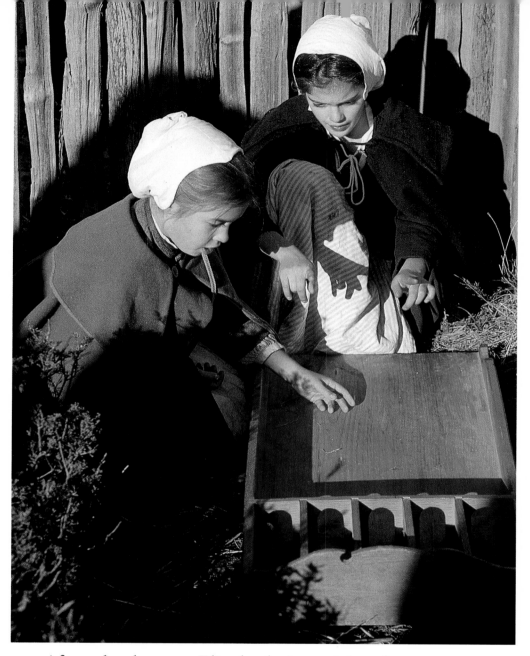

After the lesson, Elizabeth is waiting for me.
I show her my new father's gift.
He has made me a knicker box!
Elizabeth and I take turns shooting.
We keep score with scratches in the sand.
Today my marbles go through the arches more truly.
Hers bounce back to her.
I am winning, but the sun is beginning to lower
and I must get back to my chores.

I feed the fire to heat the
pottage again, and milk the
goats once more.

The big brown goat is
troublesome.

The more I push, the more
she kicks.

I will have a mark to show
from her tomorrow!

As I return from milking, my new father is coming home.

He has news of the ship.

It carries visitors to our village!

There is much talk about where to lodge them and how to portion out the stores.

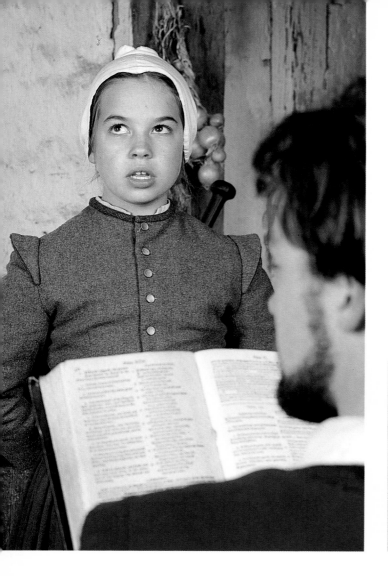

After we have eaten, my new father quizzes me on my verses.

I have been learning this one by heart since last Sabbath.

It has words to turn my tongue into a knot.

Psalm 100

A psalm for confession:
Shout ye triumphantly to Jehovah all the earth.

Serve ye Jehovah with gladness: come before him, with singing joy.

Know ye, that Jehovah he *is* God: he made us, and not we: his people, and sheep of his pasture.

Enter ye his gates, with confession; his courts with praise: confess ye to him, bless ye his name.

For Jehovah *is* good, his mercy *is* forever: and his faith, unto generation and generation.

This evening Father is pleased with my learning.
He hugs me with pride.
Perchance he does like having a daughter!

Mother calls for me.
We set off for the spring to fetch water for tomorrow.
We look out to sea and see the ship.
Perchance Mother will have letters and a bolt of new
cloth tomorrow.

Now there is time for quiet conversing.
Mother speaks first. She asks how I am
liking my new father.
I can truthfully say that I am becoming fond of him.
It has been many months since I have seen Mother
seem so glad!
The air gets chill as we fill our buckets.
It is getting towards sundown.
The village quiets as we turn homeward.

Father and Mother talk in the candlelight.
I bid them good night.

I get my bedding ready and put my overgarments in the chest.

Though I am almost grown, I tell the day's events to my poppet.

I tell her about the ship in the harbor, winning knickers from Elizabeth, and my dream.

And best of all, I tell her of my new father's pride in my learning.

It has been a fine day.

I say my prayers and thank God for his bounty.

Fare thee well.
God be with thee.

About Plimoth Plantation

Plimoth Plantation is the outdoor living museum of seventeenth-century Plymouth, Massachusetts. Visitors may explore exhibits of the *Mayflower II*, a full-scale replica of the type of ship that brought the pilgrims to the New World in 1620; the Wampanoag Indian Settlement; and the 1627 Pilgrim Village. In each of these outdoor exhibits, every effort is made to present an accurate picture of seventeenth-century life.

At the Plantation's Pilgrim Village, the year is always 1627, the date is today's. Almost seven years have passed since the first settlers left the chaos of Europe behind in order to establish their own church and to gain economic prosperity.

The modern visitor may converse with the interpreters as they go about their daily chores, which vary by season. Each interpreter has taken on the role of a real-life 1627 Plimoth resident in dress, dialect, and religious philosophy.

Within the walls of the palisade, rough-hewn and clapboard houses, each with its own kitchen garden, are set alongside an earthen street gently sloping downhill toward the ocean. Animals graze contentedly, and the smell of baking bread wafts through the air. Time is suspended as Plimoth Plantation keeps our early American heritage vibrantly alive.

Notes About the Book

Who Was Sarah Morton?

Sarah Morton was a real child. She is mentioned in several journals and histories of the period. She was nine years old in 1627.

Sarah's house had a dirt floor and was heated by one fire. The fire was right on the floor. There were tiny windows in the walls with wooden shutters. The windows let out some of the smoke from the fire, but didn't let in very much light. Her house was hot and buzzing with flies in the summer, and dark and cold in the winter. When the winters were very cold, they brought their goats and chickens inside the house to keep them from freezing.

Early settlers didn't bathe as often as we do. Sarah Morton probably had one bath a month during the warm weather, and fewer during the winter. The settlers washed their inner linens frequently, but woolen outer garments were merely brushed clean.

Although Plimoth Plantation is right on the shore of the Atlantic Ocean, people did not swim. They thought that the cold ocean water was bad for them.

When they were very hungry and food supplies were low, they would eat lobsters and other ocean fish. While they were fond of finfish, they really didn't care for shellfish and usually fed them to their pigs!

In the seventeenth century, people did not use forks to eat. If you look at the photograph of Sarah's family eating, you will see that Sarah's stepfather is using his knife to cut and eat the bread. Sarah and her family used their hands to eat food like meat and garden greens. They draped huge napkins over their shoulders to wipe their hands on.

Meet Amelia Poole

When the photographs for this book were taken, Amelia Poole was ten years old and in the fifth grade. She became interested in working at Plimoth because a friend of hers is an interpreter there. Her friend is Katherine Wheelock, who interprets the character of Elizabeth Warren.

Before Amelia began to work in the village, she read books about the period. She was given a dossier to study which included the biography of her family, and information on how to sew, play period games, and how to wear her clothes. Then she was taken into the village to begin interpreting. She spent her days with her sponsor, Jackie Duval, practicing the dialect that Sarah Morton spoke, and learning how to do her chores.

Amelia works at Plimoth three days a week during the summer, and on the weekends during the school year. She spends every day in character, going about her chores in the village. The kitchen garden needs to be planted, weeded, and harvested; animals must be taken care of; brass polished; her house swept; and food prepared.

Twentieth-century visitors wander in and out of the village homes, chat with Amelia, and watch as she goes about her day. Like all the interpreters, she always maintains her seventeenth-century character. Imagine how hard that is when a visitor asks how she liked the TV show last night, or what kind of music she likes!

When asked what her favorite aspects of interpreting are, Amelia mentions the challenge of transporting herself completely into a different time, and the contact she has with visitors from all over the world.

Glossary

Bedding—Mattress stuffed with straw 7

Churning—Making butter by hand 13

Cockerel—Rooster 6

Coif—Tight-fitting cap 6

Conversing—Talking 25

Fetch—To get 17

Game of chase—To run to catch something 9

Get the rod—To be punished . . . 13

Good day—Hello 3

Goodman—Mister or Mr. 3

Hasty pudding—Oatmeal or cornmeal cereal 8

Knickers (ka-NIK-ers)—Marbles . . 19

Mark—Bruise 20

Midday—Noon 14

Muck—Fertilizer made with straw and animal droppings 12

New World—What America was called by explorers and pilgrims . . 3

Of a sudden—All at once 16

Oh, marry!—Oh, no! or Oh, gosh! 12

Out of turn—At the wrong time or without permission 13

Overgarments—Clothes 6

Perchance—Maybe 8

Poppet—Doll 28

Portion out—Divide 21

Pottage—Thick stew 15

Sabbath—Sunday or the Lord's Day 22

Spring—Well or brook with fresh water 24

Stores—Supplies of food 21

Task—Chore 16

Tend—Take care of 8

Thee—You 3

Truly—Accurately 19

Waistcoat—Vest or jacket 7

A Seventeenth-Century Song and Three Riddles that Sarah Knew

Three Blind Mice
(sung to the traditional tune)

Three blind mice
Three blind mice
Dame Julianne
Dame Julianne
The miller and
    his merry old wife
She scraped her tripe
Lick thou the knife
Three blind mice

Who is he that
    runneth through the
hedge with his house
    on his back?

A snail.